The Bus to San Simón

& other poems

David Dayton

Boca Ciega Books
Silver Spring, Maryland

ISBN: 978-0-934184-12-0
Library of Congress Control Number: 2023936369

The following literary magazines first published the poems noted below; most have been revised to some extent, including titles:

Bachy: "A Photograph in the Morning Paper"
National Poetry Competition Winners, 1984 (Chester H. Jones Foundation): "Street Theatre"
Madrona: "The Hole in My Head"
Marilyn: "Lucid Dreaming"
New Jersey Poetry Journal: "A Visitation"; "A Poet and a Scientist Walk into a Park"
Quarry: "Nebraska Noir"
Roberson Poetry Annual: "Not Sent to My Landlord"
Southern Poetry Review: "You Looking at Me?"
Spectrum: "The Housewarming"
Tendril: "Poems Appended to Christmas Gifts"

Cover design credits: concept by David Dayton, created by 100covers.com using a Shutterstock photograph.

Boca Ciega Books is an imprint of Alembic Press.
Title page image: Auguste Préault, *Silence,* 1842–1843.
The Art Institute of Chicago. Public domain under CC0.

To my parents

Ruth Edna Bater (1925-2004)
Merritt William Dayton (1924-2020)

Their faith explained my unbelief
as owing to His inscrutable ways.
This made it possible for them to
never give up hope and still to love
as purely as parents should.

Contents

◄Playlist 1: Sorrows in Plain Sight

Doctor, my eyes have seen the years
And the slow parade of fears without crying
Now I want to understand

I have done all that I could
To see the evil and the good without hiding
You must help me if you can

—Jackson Browne
from his song "Doctor, My Eyes"

Nebraska Noir

While fishing in Harry Strunk Lake,
Dean McQuiety reeled in a foot
and then an arm with hand attached.
The detective said and I quote,
Murder is no mystery, only the motive.
The stores in McCook have sold out of handguns,
and after church there is talk.
Packed away in someone's freezer
are the heads that haven't been found.
The devil has his reasons.
He is sitting up all night
behind a hundred double-locked doors,
and at a truckstop outside Kearney
he is waiting for the next bus,
inhaling cigarettes like rations of air.

The Ragman

I've seen him at all hours in every weather,
lately bent over, lugging a duffel bag:
stocky, robust-looking white guy, graying
greased-back hair, trim salt-and-pepper beard.
Often he's puffing on a cheap briar pipe
while clenching another one in his free hand, unlit.
He carries a whole collection—their bowls
poking from all four pockets of his jeans.

Before he got the duffel bag,
he wore a Boy Scout backpack
overstuffed with what I assumed were rags
that he collected on his rounds.
So I named him The Ragman.
Then one day I saw him
pull a sweater out and put it on,
and realized that's his wardrobe he lugs around.

At one time I wished he had a little dog
to traipse along on his endless hikes.
Seeing him in yellow slicker and cap,
oblivious to the rain on a cold day in March,
I took my wish back.

Just off from work, hours after midnight,
I saw him seated at attention
on a bench in front of Tompkins County Trust.
I don't think he really saw me

skulking briskly past his blank gaze.

What with the root-smell of spring
strong on this first warm night in months,
I had the urge to greet him, maybe stop and chat.
I was afraid he might get scared and slink away,
or worse, seize my face with his eyes
and start spitting out his crazed distress.

At a safely shadowed distance, I hurried past
and still caught the germ of his loneliness.

The Housewarming

When we first moved in
we found cigarette butts everywhere,
columns of flaky ash marking the spots
where the old lady dropped them
and then forgot, or maybe just couldn't find.

The landlord said she smoked
four or five packs a day.
She lost her husband the year before last
and now she's going blind.
He showed us the chair that almost burned up
and several charred patches on the carpet.

He finally convinced her son
to move her into a nursing home.
I'm pretty sure it has linoleum floors.

They sent a man to pick up her things.
We showed him the black dress
with the note taped to the hanger that said:
"This is the dress I want to be buried in."

We've scrubbed and painted the bedroom
and kitchen. That ugly nicotine layer
on the wallpaper though: that's going to be a chore.
Those blotches of white with tails
are where the cleaning spray cut through.

Anyway, the place is beginning to feel like ours.
Although, whenever we go out for a while,
that lovely faint smell seeps back in.
When we get home, the first thing we do
is open the windows and air the place out.
We think of it as chasing away her ghost.

Evening Rush at the Safeway

Humming along with the Muzak,
I check my list, scan shelves,
and navigate the floating
archipelago of grocery carts.
An eggplant's funhouse sheen
lampoons me into child-like
embrace of the here and now,
which lasts until I see
a pouting girl defy her mother's "No!"
by hugging a box of cereal.

At the registers, I wheel my cart
into line and bump it—just barely—
into a frail-looking old man
who cranes to face me, nodding and
smiling to pardon as I apologize.
His short, swept-back hair
looks fluffy as down; the collar
of his shirt spreads gull wings
against a blazer's blue sky.

His dazzled gaze turns away.
I watch him watching the world
it takes all kinds to make
lined up behind their provisions
impatient to get home and eat.

Everyone looks on edge except him.

It's then I notice he's not behind a cart.
The magazine he's holding must be an excuse.
He's here just to take part, to see
and be seen, and maybe even touched,
if only by accident.

A toddler seated in a cart next to us
can't take it anymore and begins to wail.
The old man looks down at him,
grinning like a goofy saint.
The boy, sniffling, calms,
stares up, amazed by the gargoyle.

Flashback

Stepping from cool interior gloom
onto the glaring patio, I'm briefly
overcome, raise a hand to my brow
as though sunlight were an angel
saying, *Lo!* Near my feet are
luminous tulips, amethyst petals
forming scarlet-tipped chalices.
My hostess, like a gigantic moth
in her billowy orange dress,
flutters from blossom to bloom,
pausing to dandle and sniff.
I toddle behind, polite smile
disguising faint dread.
What is it? *The heat and wine
plus jet lag?* I don't feel able to close
against a swoony sensory overload.
My jaws clamp against a painful
shiver at the root of my tongue.
For an instant, I am one
with the purple iris I bow to examine.
Upright, I drift, helpless to catch
what she's nattering on about,
her face a grotesque mask.
Just as I think I will have to confess
that I'm ill and ask to lie down,
another inner uprush looms.
I feel my little boat tilt—*oh please god no*—
but then the wave mercifully deflates

and I ride over the crest.
I come ashore with a few dry compliments.
While she works the sliding door
after I've fumbled the tricky latch,
she asks if I'd like another drink.
I glance at the reflected garden
through my squint-pathetic face.
"Just iced tea if you have any. Thanks."

Street Theatre

A Dodge, turning left, waits under the light.
Snow tires (in June) and mud say *farmer,* poor
but practical savant—crumpled rear door
welded shut. Behind it, wearing a mite
too much make-up, his daughter leers outright,
seductress enticing you to adore.
Poker-faced, you figure: a sophomore
virgin tired of waiting for her night.
She needs the counsel of Juliet's nurse,
reads *True Romance.* Yearning to get carried
away, she tried out this sultry broadcast,
a test your bluff smile mocks. Mouthing a curse,
she gives you the finger. You've been married
and divorced before the car lurches past.

You Looking at Me?

I'm tired of keeping my eyes
tethered to the same old roads,
seeing so much of so little of life
through a windshield.
I keep spying on my kids in the rearview,
sneaking peeks like they're strangers on a bus:
ear buds plugged in, eyes glued to phone screens,
their thumbs poised, then furiously tapping.

Yesterday, my oldest—somber, concerned—
asked what I'll do after they leave
to be on their own. I joked:
"You're moving out someday? You promise?
I'm sure your dad and I will come up with a plan."
Actually, sometimes I'm afraid of what I see—
me: bored loony in a spotless house,
wiping that freaking hall mirror again
like I'm trying to erase myself.

—Oh, you don't want to hear this!
Poor me, poor me.
But when you sneak a look at my face
in the car next to yours at a light, don't judge,
and don't pretend to feel sorry.

You've got problems of your own, clearly.

County Youth in Accident

The story in the paper got it all wrong—
wasn't how fast I was goin'
or the road bein' slick from the rain.
It was that deer, crazy young buck,
cut right in front of me.
I was drivin' as fast as I always do
'cept when the road's froze up.
But that stupid deer—I forgot everything I knew
and slammed the brakes. That was it, man.
I felt like a pilot whose engine quits.
You know? Not a goddamned thing you can do.
The Jeep swerved and skidded, flipped, and—
I blacked out after that.
Mr. Hanson found me wrapped around a tree.
Said he thought I was dead at first.
You should of seen my back—
I didn't know a bruise could be huge like that.
The trooper said I must of smashed
through the windshield back-first,
though no one's figured how I could fit.
My mom swears it was a miracle.
Providence, she calls it. I call it luck, pure luck.
My dad just said he wasn't buyin' another car
for me to wreck. He didn't have to.
With what I already had in the bank, the insurance
gave me enough to buy Ed Junior's Firebird.
I take that road to work and back.
Every time, coming into that curve, it's strange—

my foot pops off the gas right where it happened.
You know the chrome rim around a windshield?
Look for it next time you drive out that way.
Funnier'n hell, all bent up, still hangin'
in the branches of that goddamned tree.

A Photograph in the Morning Paper

Like jumping
for the first time

off the high dive at the pool
when she was six,

she finally just closed her eyes
and hopped,

                  sat down in the air
knees bent

one hand trailing loose
above her head

the other hand
pinching her nose.

I later recalled
with a startled grimace

how cruel it seemed
that her puffed cheeks

held on so fiercely
to the last breath.

Night Watch

Restless, numb after too much television,
I decided to take a walk. Noiselessly,
I pulled the back door shut, slipped from
air conditioned chill into the humid air.
The strange neighborhood looked familiar,
distilled to its shadows and silhouettes,
a rerun of all the neighborhoods I used to prowl
after sneaking out my bedroom window—
modest, neatly spaced houses slumbering
in the semi-murk secured by streetlights,
a few porches lit like guardposts
beyond bristly, crew-cut lawns.
Feeling compelled to broadcast my innocence,
I strolled with my hands in my pockets,
alert behind a mask of unconcern.
My business in being out so late
was only questioned once, by a startled cat.
She arched and hissed at me, then scurried off.
I envied the privilege of her furtiveness,
felt like ducking into the pitch black
of some backyard just to feel my heart race.
I kept to the well-lit concrete path,
encountered only one other insomniac.
I heard water hissing, saw a stream
across the sidewalk and looked around. A face
flared orange in the glow of a cigarette:
puffy, rumpled face of a white, middle-aged man.
I held my look open, but he didn't glance

from the pristine turf, over which
he dully waved a fine, efficient mist.
Back at my father's porch, I sat on a step,
pulling around me the portion of darkness
I could savor without fear of trespass.
The yard I'd neglected to mow looked inviting, cool,
so I knelt and eased myself down.
Chin resting on my crossed arms, I shut my eyes
and searched for the scent of soil and roots,
imagined all the disappearing bodies underneath,
relentlessly feeding the lawns in this land of sleep.

◄Playlist 2: Ithaca, Town & Country

And it's just a box of rain
I don't know who put it there
Believe it if you need it
Or leave it if you dare

—Robert Hunter
from "Box of Rain" by the Grateful Dead

Eyes Are Incorrigible Optimists

Ever notice how at dusk in late autumn
your eyes, alarmed by the early dark,
begin to home in on lighted windows, flitting
to their glow as eagerly as sparrows to corn?
What they get usually is
disappointment so routine you hardly notice:
a glimpse of someone reading or cooking,
children silhouetted by a TV screen,
or not even that—a room as emptily lit
as your eyes are, just looking.

But often enough, never enough,
a random glance snares some delight:
a young ballerina twirling in slow motion,
fingers touching overhead: brown skin,
red leotards, black hair pulled back
so tight it gleams: her leg kicks up
impossibly high, slowly descends,
then gazelle-like she leaps,
leaving you agape at the pale ceiling
of a dance school two floors up.
You'd never noticed it before.
It's on your way home from work, so that
time and again now time stops—
at the last second before turning the corner
you find yourself looking up and back:
hopeful, expectant.

A Visitation

Biking downtown on a bright, gusty day,
a merry-making chemical in my brain,
or planetary conjunction, or God knows
what all elevates my good mood into
a natural—and thus inexplicable—high,
a wave of joy that crests as I coast, braking
as lightly as I dare down East Buffalo Street.
Through tears (bliss or wind) I evangelize
the one true way—silently, eyes appealing
to each passerby: *Rejoice!* When I spot
a friend rapt in his own thoughts I greet him
in mine with a Whitmanesque *Camerado!*
and sail by without hollering, my smile
the bars of some blessed angel's hoosegow.

Late April Afternoon

Grateful for the errand that's
put me on this rolling back road,
I'm almost convinced that it's really spring.
Through glass, the bright sun's warm.
The wooded hills shimmer: gauzy light green.

Still a good ways off, I notice an old man
backing out the door of a farmhouse.
I see him clearly as he turns,
his skull-stark face a shock
offset by the way he's dressed:
sport shirt buttoned at the jowls,
his cardigan a dapper match.

He looks plenty spry,
the part in his slicked-down hair
straight as the furrows he used to plow.
Just as I'm passing by
he steps from the sagging porch,
throws his beak up and, squint-blind,
aims a gap-toothed grin at the sun—
his death mask cracked open like an eggshell.

Not Sent to My Landlord

A lull in our sidewalk chat: You eyed
the gnarled pear tree profusely
in blossom, rejuvenated it seemed
by the crude pruning of February's ice storm.
"Time to get out the chainsaw," you said.
"Meant to cut the old girl down before now."

I was tongue-tied for a long moment.
"Really? It's a little lopsided but still...quite lovely."
You smiled as though reminded of a joke
you couldn't hold back.
Yes, you'd kept the tree around
to add a little bit of...*charm.*
You savored the word. Then eyed me frankly.
"Don't want more branches falling,
and the fruit's only good for attracting varmints."

I stood there, tight-lipped, wishing I had
my wife's exuberant hands and the moxie
to argue at least for a seasonal reprieve.
What could I have said, seeing you unmoved
by effulgent flowers quavering in the breeze
and delicate petals strewn around our feet?

I guess I could have changed the topic,
asked about your promise to get more gravel
for the steepest part of the driveway,
a safety issue, right?

With several such requests, maybe
I could have made the tree one of those chores
you keep postponing until you forget.

One night last fall, after a rainstorm stripped bare
every tree in the yard, I stood on my way inside
looking at the full moon. Turning around,
I was dumbstruck by the pear tree's transformation:
a sparkling frozen fountain of blackened branches;
at the tip of every drooping twig a glistening droplet.

I have that memory of the tree as a blessing now.
May you have its sprouting roots to worry about.

The Green Gardener's Nightmare

My wife wanted to plant a salad garden
on the slope behind the house,
at the edge of the woods, in a gap
overgrown with dock and orchard grass.
All one beaming May afternoon
I reared my uncle's pickaxe wobblingly overhead,
heaved and hung on till its evil spike thudded.
Every few strokes I'd change tools,
shove the spading fork into crevices,
stomp down, and lever up clumps of sod.

Sitting like a child in a sandbox,
my wife shook, slapped, and plied soil from roots
while I crouched and tossed aside shale,
bedrock shards a glacier dumped here.
I poked with a trowel for root-blocking slabs
and pried them out.
The moist, clayey dirt had a dead man's grip.

When I stood to get my wind,
my back stayed slightly hunched.
My blurry eyes throbbed.
I stared at the veins bulged out like mole tunnels
on my arms, the fine hair flecked with grit.
Wiping my brow, I hissed a rough equivalent
of the oath Adam blurted, eyes stung shut by sweat.

After a meal and steaming bath: sublime indolence.

In bed we massaged each other's back,
spreading almond oil, kneading the muscles
upward along the spine, at the neck
squeezing out exquisite synaptic fireworks.

When she turned over, I stayed
straddling her thighs,
spellbound by her glow in the candle's aureole.
I ate her mouth like a plum,
teased her nipples taut.
Clergy of an erotic cult,
we cast out the demon Work.

Mired in half-sleep, I came to,
focused close-up on a plot of freshly dug ground,
saw the grains of soil stirring.
Instinctively, I backed away. Then, understood:
something buried was struggling to rise.

I watched a soil-crusted human form
lift head, shoulders, torso and
collapse, eaten by the earth.
Startled, I lifted myself
and felt
myself
slip
out.

A Poet and a Scientist Walk into a Park

    "What kind of tree is that?"

What am I, a botanist?
Anyone can see it's...it's
an eye-popping throwback to May
blooming amid June's ho-hum green,
some exotic ornamental festooned
with pink blossoms, willowy boughs
swaying like a hula dancer's grass skirt.

In short:
    "I don't know."

And good thing, too.
Without a name to loosen
beauty's grip, we simply gape,
get close to smell and touch,
aping the first minds knocked up
by divine intercourse.

In the spell's afterglow, walking away:
    "I wonder what it could be?"

Language—our love-child.
    "You still don't know?"

Hermes whispered from the wings just then:
    "A whooping willow."

Reading on My Lunch Hour

A truly good book attracts very little favor to itself.
It is so true that it teaches me better than to read it.
I must soon lay it down and commence living on its hint.
— Henry David Thoreau, from his journal, February 19, 1841

On a bench facing the park's concrete plaza
I alternate reading and spectating. My eyes
need to rest from the bright white pages.

My erratic concentration seems to match the style
of the writing I'm trying to appreciate:
Robert Bly's *The Morning-Glory: Prose Poems.*

Sentences flow like the people passing by,
most barely making an impression, then suddenly
there's a spark of recognition or surprise.

"How weird the goalies seem in their African masks!"
A honeybee lands beside me on the bench,
sides aquiver, as though catching its breath.

What a nice vest: its favorite color,
velvety pollen yellow. The bee lifts off.
After some hovering indecision,

it begins to inspect the shrub behind my bench,
a prickly bush that could use some pruning,
its new growth shaggy as Einstein's mane.

Laying the book aside, I squirm around
to keep tabs on the bee, which bobs up, zips
out of sight. Gingerly, I grab a branch,

pick apart inch-long ellipsoid leaves
to pluck a tiny, lime-green kernel,
a little coincidence I dandle—

it's the exact same shape, nearly the color
of the *sake* bottle my potter sister praised
on our recent tour of the Johnson Museum.

Her exuberant awe boomeranged
to despair. Such a beautifully spare pot
required hands and mind at one

with the gnosis of essential forms
graspable everywhere in nature but requiring
years of unsparing discipline to master.

How many years of a life, how many
centuries of a culture did that simple bottle
represent? How many eons of earth-time

this seed I drop into my pocket?
(The next letter my sister gets from me
will carry a palpably cryptic P.S.)

I close my eyes and lift my face to the sun,
thinking of Thoreau, that passage in *Walden*

where he explains that sometimes

he had to leave off hoeing his beanfield
and just let everything—most of all his own
meddlesome mind—just let everything be.

Instructions for a First Visit to the Reservoir

Any hot day will do, but the ideal
would be some morning after a thunderstorm
when the sun's blazing and the sky's washed
clean as a pair of bleached blue jeans.
Take Slaterville Road out of town about half a mile
to that clearing just past the fresh produce stand.
It's likely some cars will already be parked there.
Follow the edge of the cornfield to the woods
and look for a path through the berry bramble.
Halfway downhill you'll hit a trail
running parallel to the creek. Go townward.
It's not a hike for bare feet or flip flops.
Be careful on that high, jutting turn
when you stop to catch your breath and
squint down at the glinting water.
Once up the smaller rise and out of the woods
you'll see another path straight downhill
to where the creek feeds into the reservoir.
The leaning weeds will lash,
making your legs itch.
In your rush for the water don't take
a wrong turn among the cattails,
and don't expect us to take any notice
as you wade the creek by that uprooted stump.
If you're lucky there'll be plenty of room
on the gravelly island for you to lay down a towel

and strip. You'll want to get in the water quick,
but wade in slowly—it'll be cold at first.
Breaststroke out a ways, getting used to it.
When you come out, a newly baptized member
of our congregation, you'll feel a little self-conscious.
Lie down and let the sun cure what ails you,
mind melting into skin.
We'll chat, swim, and bask all afternoon;
imagining at moments we're in the Caribbean,
the crows heard as macaws,
the shouts and splashing from across the lagoon
more of our tribe, playing.

One last thing:
if folks suddenly grab up their clothes
and hightail-it for the woods, do likewise.
You can bet cops are marching down the trail,
grim and implacable as conquistadors.

Evening Performance

On her way across the yard
our plump calico stops,
plunks her butt down
and gives her breast fur
a few dainty licks.

Having stolen the scene from
the sunset, she makes a show
of sniffing the grass and then
pretends to be intrigued
by quavering leaf shadows.

She peers at the horizon's
lavish conflagration of colors.
Unimpressed, she saunters to the fence.

I'm sitting in the porch swing,
veteran stagehand
who always dreamed of one day being
Director.

I push off the ground lightly
and lean back
into the swing's wooden slats.

The chains creak above me,
rusty pulleys slowly drawing closed
a diaphanous curtain.

House lights come on.
Bowing into a sudden breeze, I stand up,
and hear the applause of the maple trees.

Lucid Dreaming

I've mounted my bicycle and pedaled into the street
when I realize I'm the emperor without clothes.

Panicked, I begin to pee on my leg.
But after all, it's raining. I'm dreaming.
No sweat.
Riding along this way is goofy bliss.

Ahead I see where the bridge has washed out.
A wave curls up and looms above me.
After lightning before thunder booms.

Absurdly, I think I can still get across.
I pedal full-speed, embracing sheer air
like the pilot of an early flying machine.

The water's warm soup.
How stupid of me.

I fish up the bike by its handlebars
and pull for shore using a modified sidestroke.

Climbing out, I'm grinning like a capsized drunk.
My wife already awake asks,
"What? What are you so happy about?"

◀Playlist 3: Fides Poetica

I have spent my life
Seeking all that's still unsung
Bent my ear to hear the tune
And closed my eyes to see
When there were no strings to play
You played to me

—Robert Hunter
from "Attics of My Life" by the Grateful Dead

Polistes

The wasps that kept us alert
in and out the door all summer
stir in my mind as I handle their nest,
wing blur whirling them lazily away,
their legs—jointed black and topaz threads—
dangling beneath menacing abdomens.

In late May
the nest mushroomed from the eaves,
a gray, upside-down toadstool
attended by two single-minded wasps.
They were far enough away to leave alone
but close enough to watch.
In the natural sciences I am a tourist,
so I checked out a guidebook:
The Social Insects.

By mid-July
the nest resembled a champagne glass,
effervescent with newly hatched workers—
robots, according to the book,
programmed by genes to obey chemicals
that attendants lick off the queen.
Their communication system was designed
by the genius that put pleasure in sex:
when fed, larvae secrete a milky goo
adults crave and pass mouth to mouth,
a communal addiction that governs workflow,

triggering the queen's directives
literally through feedback.

Scabrous, unbelievably light,
the nest enchants my fingertips.
Among empty cells
five domed ones constellate a star.
They blur when I twirl the stem
and the thing becomes a mandala,
emblem of Cosmos—the human nest—
a people's single-mindedness
woven of ritual and myth,
scripture and faith, and for some
but not us—politics.
I recall Norman O. Brown
lecturing on Pound's *Cantos,*
chagrinned because he could not salvage
for his freedom-loving students
the word *totalitarian.*

The domed cells entomb pupae.
At the ragged end of her rope of ovaries,
the queen grew comatose, cold.
Workers stopped feeding the larvae
then abandoned the nest.
Males mated and died.
Young females packed sperm and fled.
They alone survive the winter,
sheltered under bark,
in beams of outbuildings, crevices of rock.
You'll see them flying around

sluggishly in early spring,
amnesiacs remembering.
A good hot day will bring it all back—
nectar will be right where they left it.

Polistes always build from scratch,
unable to use an old nest—
one of the infinite, minute mysteries
that feed entomologists.
I found this one in a footnote:
workers that desert the nest in early fall
may find a sunny spot on a wall somewhere
and, individually, pulp wood
with manic drive before cold kills them,
repeating all the motions of building a nest.
Severed from the queen's intelligence
they can only construct splotches of carton
that have no apparent use, though
a waspish prof I know would call them
an endgame, their postmodern art.

Pauper's Tale

For W.S. Merwin

here I am again
begging words on the corner where silence passes
looking the other way

and to think I could be a rich man

if I could count the times
the wind has emptied its pockets
saying take what you want

well I have my pride

For Father Raymond Roseliep

(And Sobi-Shi, his haiku-writing alter ego.)

bumblebees bounce off
his lily-white tennis shoes
blooming in clover

stuck stone flips over
sowbugs minding their business
what is it they do

dodging a swallow
his eyes crash into a ditch
heap of feathers, ash

Sobi-Shi at dusk
lifts fireflies in a jar
waits for the moonrise

as his eyes eat words
the cat in his lap watches
a mosquito dance

he yawns suddenly
stares at his bare foot's profile
the maternal curves

under shooting stars
Sobi-Shi smiles, wet brush poised
unfinished is best

Poems Appended to Christmas Gifts

For Mom

This odd windchime made of stone,
pearl- and ocher-whorled slices
of agate dangling from a drift-
wood stick worn smooth as bone.

Hang it in a window till
spring to adorn the view
of bare trees, gray sky, snow.
All winter let it be still

except when you daydream,
warming the chimes with breath
to hear icicles crackling,
the clear trickle of a stream.

In May hang it from the eaves
near the porch swing and enjoy
the random jingling, music
for light shimmering through leaves.

For Dad

This cherrywood carving of the laughing Buddha:
bald, basset-eared, with the paunch
of a woman nine months pregnant.
My impulse-buyer's wish
was that you'd make him a household god—
just kidding, of course.
Call him a joke, or a charm.
Pat his belly often enough
and maybe you'll find
yourself with his zany grin,
eyebrows arched like leaping dolphins.
The sleeves of his gown
trail from his upraised arms, his hands bent back
as though he were the Orient's Atlas,
supporting the heavens—such a light illusion—
on his fingertips.
He could have tutored Solomon.
Take his advice:
Try softer.
Put your shoulder to the pillow,
your nose to a flower.
Want not; what's needed comes.
An idle mind is the Buddha's playground.

A Birthday Poem for Emily

Winter is an Occupation—
Fit Calling for the Soul—
Attending the daily Funeral
Pacifies the Will—while
The stark Simplicity of View—
Nurtures the Metaphysical.
Walled by Meditation
One's Burrow seems
Sublime—and then—
Sunlight through a Window—
Resurrects the Skin.

The Hole in My Head

For Charles Simic

Somewhere back of my eyes
I can feel the hole in my head
dropping like a mine shaft into my body.

Thought circles this hole
like an Eskimo,
harpoon half-cocked, or late at night like a drunk
tottering, one foot scuffing stones
over the brink.

When I look at a snapshot of myself,
I try to find what's always left out
behind the bluff smile,
the inane stare blank as an electric outlet.

The hole in my head
glows blue-white at the edges,
a ring of phosphorescent cells,
a toothless mouth
that swallows each moment,
even now sucking in these words,
returning intact
the skeletons of tiny fish.

With John Gill at the Elysian Fields Café

1.

You're gaunt as Gauguin's *Yellow Christ,*
John, and your iconoclasm is so ingrained
I see you're cringing at that comparison.

You sure you can't see it?
We could get you a sexy loin cloth,
hire the hippie carpenters at Knock-on-Wood
to make a splinter-free white-pine cross.

Of course, you couldn't have
the autumnal hills of Brittany behind you
and no women in nun-like garb
kneeling underneath,
just a stubbled, hardscrabble cornfield and maybe
a few goth nerds from Tburg High.

Okay. Let me try again.

You're gaunt as Abe Lincoln, John,
who grew his famous beard
because a young girl's letter
apprised him that his cheeks looked so cadaverous
he was scaring folks.

You told me your author's photo
on the back cover of *Country Pleasures*

scared you so much you forthwith
shaved off that fleecy beard.
It wasn't the beard, John.
Lincoln couldn't do much about
the twin gravestones of his eyes,
and in that photograph yours are bulging and fierce
as John Brown's in the raid on Harpers Ferry.

You got rid of the shaggy face fringe
hoping nobody'd recognize the solitary abolitionist
who railed sermons at winter trees.
"Free the slaves of love!
Unlock the hope-forged manacles
of their hopeless bondage!"

What do you mean, "That's a little too weird"?
Okay, I'll take one more crack at it.
The plain-spoken truth this time:

You're gaunt as a scarecrow
in the unprized vineyard of American poetry,
John.

I see Poe's inscrutable, gimlet-eyed raven
has settled on the floppy brim
of your rakishly cocked, Whitmanesque hat.
Try not to look so grim, okay?
Kick up your heels and flap those spindly arms!
Dance the sonofabitch away
in your own eccentric wind.

2.

You step from the porch of your ramshackle house
in the sun-pierced coolness just after dawn
and head off with Sasha, ambling through weeds
into that remnant of wilderness
along the rim of Taughannock gorge.

Sasha wanders off behind her nose,
tethered to your calls as you lope the swerving trail
down to that outcropping on the cliff face
near the falls, a hermit's throne
that gives you the illusion when you sit down
of being suspended in the slate-walled chasm.

You pull your legs into full-lotus
and stare at the frothy white torrent
plunging straight down over 200 feet.
You feel eerily down-drawn
but held up by your rigid backbone.

Closing your eyes, you let the cataract's white noise
be your first mantra and focus on the third-eye chakra.
You begin the ritual breathing routines that calm
and carry your mind deeper into meditation.
Soon that tingling at the base of your spine
begins to rise, the *prana* surging through.
Ek Ong Kar Sat Gur Prasad.
"The creator and the creation are one.
All is a blessing of the one creator."

***

Timeless time passes the instant you recognize
Sasha's barking, calling you back
to your self, your place,
your life.

To Bernice Atwater Dayton

Days past peak bloom,
the rose I brought home
still comforts the eyes
its exuberant red loosened, enlarged.
A few of the petals, half
shriveled, cling to the sepal,
their career of slow
curling outward nearly
done. Soon enough,
air stirred by a shut door
will bring them all down.
Until then, we will leave this rose
to center the room,
marveling at how it
fountains from each now
into the next, ever-changing
and yet holding, like
the nimbus of memory
around a grandmother's face,
the steady radiance of its being:
sweet bud to fecund bloom
to this exhausted survivor
giving and giving itself
to the ravishing air.

A Christmas Poem, 1980

For John Lennon

Thermostat down, the kitchen light off,
I strip and crawl into bed, shivering.
Nancy starts, without fully waking
smiles and takes me into her warmth.
I bask like a sated infant, growing
drowsy, sucking a dream-nipple.
Floating to mind: the defiant self-sufficiency
of the old Italian man staring from
the front page of a recent *Daily News.*
He and his neighbors refused orders
to leave their quake-demolished town.
He sat tending a fire, his little
granddaughter standing near, bundled up.
A luxury hotel room on the coast?
His soul would be corpse-cold by spring.
Let him sit in the open, near the rubble
of the village that mothered him, family
gathered around whatever they can find
to burn, and he'll glow, scheming, figuring
two years, with help maybe one...

Yesterday I browsed Christmas cards,
looking for the Nativity I'd begun
to imagine. All the ethereal depictions
made me wish Käthe Kollwitz had drawn
the mother of god. Her Madonna, like mine,

would be plain-looking, a peasant woman
worn out by her first labor, straw sticking
to her hair, eyes showing joyful relief
as she wipes the blood off his cheeks.
No halos, just the stable's cozy aura.
The shit dropping from the oxen steams!

I wonder what it would take to teach the men
who hold the world hostage compassion?
Suppose I transport the Soviet Premier
and our President-elect, both in deepest sleep,
and lay them down together in a hayloft.
Each draws toward the other as they recall
in simultaneous dreams the previous lives
when they hid out in the same barn,
deserters from opposing armies, comrades in
desperation who had no language to bind them
and eyed each other with edgy mistrust
but at night lay down as matter-of-factly
as lovers and hugged under their blankets,
shivering, until their mothering heat
embraced them and they slept. Suppose
precisely at the end of their dream the cries
of all the babies born that instant wake them.

◄*Playlist 4: There You Are*

Reach out your hand, if your cup be empty
If your cup is full, may it be again
Let it be known there is a fountain
That was not made by the hands of men

—Robert Hunter
from "Ripple" by the Grateful Dead

He's in Mexico Writing a Novel

All morning he sits in his little room
at a book- and paper-strewn table,
mostly gazing at the sun-flooded courtyard.
Just outside the window a fat rose dangles,
floppy dollop of yellow.
Under the little apricot tree,
a gangly geranium splatters scarlet
against the shady white wall.

A motorcycle revs up next door.
The greenhouse workers are breaking for lunch.
Their banter makes him envious.
He scans a page of typescript, chagrinned
by the nearly unreadable words he has penned
between lines and in the margins.
Deciding to seek some fellowship and food,
he gets up, grabs his wallet and cowboy hat.

It's a short walk to the bus stop.
He lets his eyes roam the stubbled fields,
an expanse of desiccated light tan
broken up by the greens of cactus, maguey,
and tall dusty eucalyptus.
The usual bluish haze blurs the far-off hills.

At the corner he sits down on a patch of grass
on the crest of the irrigation ditch,
back hunched to the sun. He asks

the *campesino* standing in the wall's scant shade
when the bus will come. The man
squints down the washboard road,
answers with the all-purpose sing-song shrug:
"Quién sabe?"
They trade grins.
He asked just to hear it said.

A low black Trans Am rumbles by,
tough-looking *hombre* at the wheel,
super-cool though bouncing in slow motion.
From the corner of his eye he watches
the *campesino* watch the chalky dust waft away,
thankful for small blessings like being upwind.
Down the side street,
an old guy's dipping a tin cup into a *maguey*,
checking the sap for a batch of homebrew.
He recalls that ponderous line from *Man's Fate:*
"There is always a need for intoxication."

A descending jet's sonorous roar
shakes the imaginary beer he's raised.
American Airlines 727, landing gear down,
about ten minutes from the Mexico City airport.
He imagines the best sellers being tucked away,
their florid titles glinting metallic ink...
He wonders if he could still get his old job back,
that comfy niche in the work-a-day world,
a decent paycheck every two weeks.

A *muchacho* rides past on an old bike,

a hand-me-down he doesn't quite fit.
He has to pedal standing up, lurching
from side to side as he lifts his crotch
back and forth over the crossbar.
He began with a running leap and now
his ambition's a necessary faith, sustained
so long as he keeps pumping those pedals.
Our hero watches him fade into the glow
of metaphor, hears the bus's clutch slip and grind.
He stands up, adjusts his hat to shade his eyes,
and saunters over to where, *más o menos,*
the bus door will open.

The House of Little Smiles

Mellow after a long shower
I sit down in the living room for a few minutes
before fixing dinner.

I think how banal the moment is in English:
the housekeeper taking a break.
"So you're the mistress of the house,"
my neighbor teased, and I grinned,
nodding proudly, having misheard *el ama* as
el alma de casa, "the soul of the house"—
a designation I've decided to keep.

Now that I've dusted, swept, mopped,
vacuumed, and tidied up,
mowed, pruned, weeded, and raked,
I collect my wages.

The square white coffee table glistens.
Toward one corner I've put a garnet vase
filled with purple bougainvillea,
decanted distillation of the teeming yard,
whose trim I admire through a window that is,
if I say so myself, pellucid.

I'm ready to draw up my *Plan de San Simón*,
establishing this house as a sovereign nation.
I see we already have a flag—

the wild morning-glory unfurled a blossom
from the pole where our little gate bell dings,
its cord yanked by a partisan breeze.

Two lizards in file scurry and stop, scurry and stop
along the top of the yard's high wall.
They can be our border patrol.

Spanish Lesson

My hand rests on her sheeted hip,
glides down the naked slope,
mounts her back.

She's hunting my word for the day,
sifting a random page
of our thick black *Cassell's.*

"Ok," she says: "*cerro:*
neck of an animal; backbone,
ridge formed by the backbone;

also: hill, high land."

Letting it sink in,
I wonder the connection.

My instructing finger skims down her spine.
Dawn. The rolling hills we jog toward.

The Bus to San Simón

Motor groaning through a muffler that's more like
a microphone, this village jalopy lurches and rocks,
rattling along at a jaunty burro's pace.
Both hands clutching the luggage rack,
I sway in the crowded aisle.
We standing hover like sulky ghosts
above those with seats, the lucky ones
complacently oblivious to us.
The young man I'm hanging over is
in another world, transported there
by a pocket-size comic book.
I can't follow the dialogue balloons,
but I don't need a dictionary to translate
the pictures: A man and a woman,
gravely prim in Gay 90s high-fashion,
stroll in a park, blotting out the scenery
with their conversation, sentences
that dwindle to phrases as they walk along
and end with the woman's
¡¿Qué—?!
as the man grabs her into his arms.
In the last panel her parasol is falling
as she, grabbing him back, surrenders to his kiss.
Behind them there's a question mark encased
in a halo like a saint.
Naturally, I'm eager for the page to turn,
but my page-turner turns around instead, kissed
by something he just remembered.

Peering worriedly past my hip, he asks:
¿Está bien?
I look under my arm at a couple across the aisle
perched on the edge of their seat,
arms draped over the seat in front
to brace the shoulders of their twins,
identically pretty little girls,
their light-brown skin and straight black hair
made even lovelier by identical pink dresses.
Their closed eyes and drooping heads answer.
Está bien, the man mutters, sheepishly,
and settles back to his comic book.
The parents, evidently his guests,
hold shyly proud smiles over the heads
of their sleeping beauties. I smile, too,
feeling less like a ghost now than
guardian angel.

I'm still feeling a bit ethereal
when I get off the bus, alone.
It's a quarter mile to the house, on another dirt road,
passing prickly pear and century plants,
behind them cornfields—
bucolic mess of stubble and piled-up stalks.
In the plain light of day
it's a hard landscape to like, close-up.
But twilight has erased thorns, manure, dead dogs,
the trash in the roadside ditch.
The chalky dust that covers everything
has become a faint, silvery luminescence,
thanks to the moon, just-risen above

the eastern rim of hills.

A nearly full moon, amazingly large,
in an equally incredible, peacock-blue sky.

I'm enchanted, of course, but also
mocked by skeptical detachment.
Meaning to be wisely wry,
I ask the moon:
¿Está bien?

The question boomerangs.
The sleeping child is mine.

Pure stupid joy pours in.

¡Ya! corazón.

It's only for a now that won't last long, but
wake up, wake up.

We're home.

Playa Azul, Michoacan

We trudge across the deserted beach
like Canadians caught without snowshoes
until at last our feet slap wet sand.
A rangy mutt trots ahead of us into the surf
gushing around him like spilled beer.
He sniffs and laps gingerly with his slack tongue.

I think he's the reincarnation of my grandfather,
the evangelist who retired to the Jersey shore.
He seems to be enjoying his new life:
no thought of testing his faith like Peter,
he splashes through the water like any child.

After a swim we lie on our makeshift blanket,
a colorful poncho,
icy droplets pricking our skin as they dry,
leaving a salt-stiffened burn.
Half-baked,
I jump up and sprint down to the water,
lifting my knees into the surf
like a fullback plowing through tacklers.
When I'm up to my chin,
I slip out of my suit
and wave it at you to come join me.
I put it back on just as the next breaker rolls up.
I swim like mad to stay with it
then get swept forward as it breaks.

I ride that wave all the way to the sand, where you are cheering me on, your teeth gleaming like a trophy.

Sunbathing Baptism

I let the breeze unfurl my towel,
kneel as it luffs to the sand,
rub in tanning oil and lie down,
ready to regress a few million years
in the history of consciousness.
Eyes closed,
I attend my skin's celebration,
nerve ends growing giddy, warming
to one another like office party drunks.
In my eyelids' kaleidoscope
I watch a swirling, coral-colored pool
that becomes incandescent, hurts—
I sit up blinking tears,
look around, only to be light-
stung by the dazzling water.
Squeezing dark's the only balm.
I let my head fall back to the towel.
Ahh, my body's remembering origins,
an eon of basking on brine-scoured rocks—surf
BOOM
makes my heart skip,
a reflex I smile at.
Why, I'd be lucky to go like this—
the only pain such pleasant heat,
my barnacle self
dissolving in death's alembic.

Sunny Yard, Childcare

How many times on a day such as this
have I closed my eyes to focus
on the invisible?
The better to feel the sun's soothing hint of heat
through the chilly air,
the better to hear what there is to hear—
a gust making the trees
sound like waves on a shore.

How many times? And each time
the same me opening my eyes again, still here,
grateful for the frisson of sunshine and cool wind.

It makes me laugh through my eyes looking at you
little one
too new to know
and with no reason to

that the nothing you came from
and the nothing to which you will return

is here right now
hidden by everything.

www.ingramcontent.com/pod-product-compliance
Lightning Source LLC
Chambersburg PA
CBHW021143020426
42331CB00005B/875